ERNEST HEMINGWAY

ERNEST HEMINGWAY
THE LAST INTERVIEW
and OTHER CONVERSATIONS

MELVILLE HOUSE
BROOKLYN · LONDON

ERNEST HEMINGWAY: THE LAST INTERVIEW
AND OTHER CONVERSATIONS

First Melville House printing: December 2015

Melville House Publishing   8 Blackstock Mews
46 John Street   and   Islington
Brooklyn, NY 11201   London N4 2BT

mhpbooks.com   facebook.com/mhpbooks   @melvillehouse

ISBN: 978-1-61219-522-3

Library of Congress Control Number: 2015955748

Printed in the United States of America
10 9 8 7 6 5 4 3 2

CONTENTS

ERNEST HEMINGWAY, THE ART OF FICTION, NO. 21

INTERVIEW BY GEORGE PLIMPTON
THE PARIS REVIEW
MAY 1954

HEMINGWAY: You go to the races?

INTERVIEWER: Yes, occasionally.

HEMINGWAY: Then you read the Racing Form . . . There you have the true art of fiction.

—Conversation in a Madrid café, May 1954

Ernest Hemingway writes in the bedroom of his house in the Havana suburb of San Francisco de Paula. He has a special workroom prepared for him in a square tower at the southwest corner of the house, but prefers to work in his bedroom, climbing to the tower room only when "characters" drive him up there.

The bedroom is on the ground floor and connects with the main room of the house. The door between the two is kept ajar by a heavy volume listing and describing The World's Aircraft Engines. The bedroom is large, sunny, the windows facing east and south letting in the day's light on white walls and a yellow-tinged tile floor.

The room is divided into two alcoves by a pair of chest-high bookcases that stand out into the room at right angles from opposite walls. A large and low double bed dominates one section, oversized slippers and loafers neatly arranged at the foot, the two bedside tables at the head piled seven-high with books. In the other alcove stands a massive flat-top desk with a chair at either side, its surface an ordered clutter of papers and mementos. Beyond it, at the far end of the room, is an armoire with a leopard skin draped across the top. The other walls are lined with white-painted bookcases from which books overflow to the floor, and are piled on top among old newspapers, bullfight journals, and stacks of letters bound together by rubber bands.

It is on the top of one of these cluttered bookcases—the one against the wall by the east window and three feet or so from his bed—that Hemingway has his "work desk"—a square foot of cramped area hemmed in by books on one side and on the other by a newspaper-covered heap of papers, manuscripts, and pamphlets. There is just enough space left on top of the bookcase for a typewriter, surmounted by a wooden reading board, five or six pencils, and a chunk of copper ore to weight down papers when the wind blows in from the east window.

A working habit he has had from the beginning, Hemingway stands when he writes. He stands in a pair of his oversized loafers on the worn skin of a lesser kudu —the typewriter and the reading board chest-high opposite him.

When Hemingway starts on a project he always begins with a pencil, using the reading board to write on onionskin typewriter paper. He keeps a sheaf of the blank paper on a clipboard to the left of the typewriter, extracting the paper a sheet at a time from under a metal clip that reads "These Must Be Paid." He places the paper slantwise on the reading board, leans against the board with his left arm, steadying the paper with his hand, and fills the paper with handwriting which through the years has become larger, more boyish, with a paucity of punctuation, very few capitals, and often the period marked with an X. The page completed, he clips it facedown on another clipboard that he places off to the right of the typewriter.

Hemingway shifts to the typewriter, lifting off the reading board, only when the writing is going fast and well, or when the writing is, for him at least, simple: dialogue, for instance.

He keeps track of his daily progress—"so as not to kid myself"—on a large chart made out of the side of a cardboard packing case and set up against the wall under the nose of a mounted gazelle head. The numbers on the chart showing the daily output of words differ from 450, 575, 462, 1250, back to 512, the higher figure on days Hemingway puts in extra work so he won't feel guilty spending the following day fishing on the Gulf Stream..

A man of habit, Hemingway does not use the perfectly suitable desk in the other alcove. Though it allows more space for writing, it too has its miscellany: stacks of letters; a stuffed toy lion of the type sold in Broadway nighteries; a small burlap bag full of carnivore teeth; shotgun shells; a shoehorn; wood carvings of lion, rhino, two zebras, and a wart-hog—these last set in a neat row across the surface of the desk—and, of course, books: piled on the desk, beside tables, jamming the shelves in indiscriminate order—novels, histories, collections of poetry, drama, essays. A look at their titles shows their variety. On the shelf opposite Hemingway's knee as he stands up to his "work desk" are Virginia Woolf's The Common Reader, *Ben Ames William's* House Divided, The Partisan Reader, *Charles A. Beard's* The Republic, *Tarle's* Napoleon's Invasion of Russia, How Young You Look *by Peggy Wood. Alden Brook's* Shakespeare and the Dyer's Hand, *Baldwin's* African Hunting, *T. S. Eliot's* Collected Poems, *and two books on General Custer's fall at the battle of the Little Big Horn.*

The room, however, for all the disorder sensed at first sight, indicates on inspection an owner who is basically neat but cannot bear to throw anything away—especially if sentimental value is attached. One bookcase top has an odd assortment of mementos; a giraffe made of wood beads; a little cast-iron turtle; tiny models of a locomotive; two jeeps and a Venetian gondola; a toy bear with a key in its back; a monkey carrying a pair of cymbals; a miniature guitar; and a little tin model of a U.S. Navy biplane (one wheel missing) resting awry on a circular straw place mat—the quality of the collection that of the odds-and-ends which turn up in a shoebox at the back of a small boy's closet. It is evident, though, that these tokens have their value, just as three buffalo horns Hemingway keeps in his bedroom have a value dependent not on size but because during the acquiring of them things went badly in the bush, yet ultimately turned out well. "It cheers me up to look at them," he says.

Hemingway may admit superstitions of this sort, but he prefers not to talk about them, feeling that whatever value they may have can be talked away. He has much the same attitude about writing. Many times during the making of this interview he stressed that the craft of writing should not be tampered with by an excess of scrutiny—"that though there is one part of writing that is solid and you do it no harm by talking about it, the other is fragile, and if you talk about it, the structure cracks and you have nothing."

As a result, though a wonderful raconteur, a man of rich humor, and possessed of an amazing fund of knowledge on subjects which interest him, Hemingway finds it difficult to talk about writing—not because he has few ideas on the subject, but rather because he feels so strongly that such ideas should remain unexpressed, that to be asked questions on them "spooks" him (to use one of his favorite expressions) to the point where he is almost inarticulate. Many of the replies in this interview he preferred to work out on his reading board. The occasional waspish tone of his answers is also part of this strong feeling that writing is a private, lonely occupation with no need for witnesses until the final work is done.

This dedication to his art may suggest a personality at odds with the rambunctious, carefree, world-wheeling Hemingway-at-play of popular conception. The fact is that Hemingway, while obviously enjoying life, brings an equivalent dedication to everything he does—an outlook that is essentially serious, with a horror of the inaccurate, the fraudulent, the deceptive, the half-baked.

Nowhere is the dedication he gives his art more evident than in the yellow-tiled bedroom—where early in the morning Hemingway gets up to stand in absolute concentration in front of his reading board, moving only to shift weight from one foot to another, perspiring heavily when the work is going well, excited as a boy, fretful, miserable when the artistic touch momentarily vanishes—slave of a self-imposed discipline which lasts until about noon when he takes a knotted walking stick and leaves the house for the swimming pool where he takes his daily half-mile swim.

INTERVIEWER: Are these hours during the actual process of writing pleasurable?

HEMINGWAY: Very.

INTERVIEWER: Could you say something of this process?

When do you work? Do you keep a strict schedule?

HEMINGWAY: When I am working on a book or a story I write every morning as soon after first light as possible. There is no one to disturb you and is it is cool or cold and you come to your work and warm as you write. You read what you have written and, as you always stop when you know what is going to happen next, you go on from there. You write until you come to a place where you still have your juice and know what will happen next and you stop and try to live through until the next day when you hit it again. You have started at six in the morning, say, and may go on until noon or be through before that. When you stop you are as empty, and at the same time never empty but filling, as when you have made love to someone you love. Nothing can hurt you, nothing can happen, nothing means anything until the next day when you do it again. It is the wait until the next day that is hard to get through.

INTERVIEWER: Can you dismiss from your mind whatever project you're on when you're away from the typewriter?

HEMINGWAY: Of course. But it takes discipline to do it and this discipline is acquired. It has to be.

INTERVIEWER: Do you do any rewriting as you read up to the place you left off the day before? Or does that come later, when the whole is finished?

HEMINGWAY: I always rewrite each day up to the point where

I stopped. When it is all finished, naturally you go over it. You get another chance to correct and rewrite when someone else types it, and you see it clean in type. The last chance is in the proofs. You're grateful for these different chances.

INTERVIEWER: How much rewriting do you do?

HEMINGWAY: It depends. I rewrote the ending to *Farewell to Arms*, the last page of it, thirty-nine times before I was satisfied.

INTERVIEWER: Was there some technical problem there? What was it that had stumped you?

HEMINGWAY: Getting the words right.

INTERVIEWER: Is it the rereading that gets the "juice" up?

HEMINGWAY: Rereading places you at the point where it *has* to go on, knowing it is as good as you can get it up to there. There is always juice somewhere.

INTERVIEWER: But are there times when the inspiration isn't there at all?

HEMINGWAY: Naturally. But if you stopped when you knew what would happen next, you can go on. As long as you can start, you are all right. The juice will come.

INTERVIEWER: Thornton Wilder speaks of mnemonic devices

that get the writer going on his day's work. He says you once told him you sharpened twenty pencils.

HEMINGWAY: I don't think I ever owned twenty pencils at one time. Wearing down seven number-two pencils is a good day's work.

INTERVIEWER: Where are some of the places you have found most advantageous to work? The Ambos Mundos hotel must have been one, judging from the number of books you did there. Or do surroundings have little effect on the work?

HEMINGWAY: The Ambos Mundos in Havana was a very good place to work in. This Finca is a splendid place, or was. But I have worked well everywhere. I mean I have been able to work as well as I can under varied circumstances. The telephone and visitors are the work destroyers.

INTERVIEWER: Is emotional stability necessary to write well? You told me once that you could only write well when you were in love. Could you expound on that a bit more?

HEMINGWAY: What a question. But full marks for trying. You can write any time people will leave you alone and not interrupt you. Or rather you can if you will be ruthless enough about it. But the best writing is certainly when you are in love. If it is all the same to you I would rather not expound on that.

INTERVIEWER: How about financial security? Can that be a detriment to good writing?

HEMINGWAY: If it came early enough and you loved life as much as you loved your work it would take much character to resist the temptations. Once writing has become your major vice and greatest pleasure only death can stop it. Financial security then is a great help as it keeps you from worrying. Worry destroys the ability to write. Ill health is bad in the ratio that it produces worry which attacks your subconscious and destroys your reserves.

INTERVIEWER: Can you recall an exact moment when you decided to become a writer?

HEMINGWAY: No, I always wanted to be a writer.

INTERVIEWER: Philip Young in his book on you suggests that the traumatic shock of your sever 1918 mortar wound had a great influence on you as a writer. I remember in Madrid you talked briefly about his thesis, finding little in it, and going on to say that you thought the artist's equipment was not an acquired characteristic, but inherited, in the Mendelian sense.

HEMINGWAY: Evidently in Madrid that year my mind could not be called very sound. The only thing to recommend it would be that I spoke only briefly about Mr. Young's book and his trauma theory of literature. Perhaps the two concussions and a skull fracture of that year had made me irresponsible in my statements. I do remember telling you that I believed imagination could be the result of inherited racial experience. It sounds all right in good jolly post-concussion talk, but I think that is more or less where it belongs. So until the next liberation trauma, let's leave it there. Do you agree? But thanks for leaving out the names of any relatives I might have implicated. The fun of talk is to explore, but much of it and all that is irresponsible should not be written. Once written you have to stand by it. You may have said it to see whether you believed it or not. On the question you raised, the effects of wounds vary greatly. Simple wounds which do not break bone are of little account. They sometimes give confidence. Wounds which do extensive bone and nerve damage are not good for writers, nor anybody else.

INTERVIEWER: What would you consider the best intellectual training for the would-be writer?

HEMINGWAY: Let's say that he should go out and hang himself because he finds that writing well is impossibly difficult. Then he should be cut down without mercy and forced by his own self to write as well as he can for the rest of his life. At least he will have the story of the hanging to commence with.

INTERVIEWER: How about people who've gone into the academic career? Do you think the large numbers of writers who hold teaching positions have compromised their literary careers?

HEMINGWAY: It depends on what you call compromise. Is the usage that of a woman who has been compromised? Or is it the compromise of the statesman? Or the compromise made with your grocer or your tailor that you will pay a little more but will pay it later? A writer who can both write and teach should be able to do both. Many competent writers have proved it could be done. I could not do it, I know, and I admire those who have been able to. I would think though that the academic life could put a period to outside experience which might possibly limit growth of knowledge of the world. Knowledge, however, demands more responsibility of a writer and makes writing more difficult. Trying to write something of permanent value is a full-time job even though only a few hours a day are spent on the actual writing. A writer can be compared to a well. There are as many kinds of wells as there are writers. The important thing is to have good water in the well, and it is better to take a regular amount out than to pump the well dry and wait for it to refill. I see I am getting away from the question, but the question was not very interesting.

INTERVIEWER: Would you suggest newspaper work for the young writer? How helpful was the training you had with the *Kansas City Star*?

HEMINGWAY: On the *Star* you were forced to learn to write a simple declarative sentence. This is useful to anyone. Newspaper work will not harm a young writer and could help him if he gets out of it in time. This is one of the dustiest clichés there is and I apologize for it. But when you ask someone old, tired questions you are apt to receive old, tired answers.

INTERVIEWER: You once wrote in *The Transatlantic Review* that the only reason for writing journalism was to be well paid. You said: "And when you destroy the valuable things you have by writing about them, you want to get big money for it." Do you think of writing as a type of self-destruction?

HEMINGWAY: I do not remember ever writing that. But it sounds silly and violent enough for me to have said it to avoid having to bite on the nail and make a sensible statement. I certainly do not think of writing as a type of self-destruction, though journalism, after a point has been reached, can be a daily self-destruction for a serious creative writer.

INTERVIEWER: Do you think the intellectual stimulus of the company of other writers is of any value to an author?

HEMINGWAY: Certainly.

INTERVIEWER: In the Paris of the twenties did you have any sense of "group feeling" with other writers and artists?

HEMINGWAY: No. There was no group feeling. We had respect for each other. I respected a lot of painters, some of my own age, others older—Gris, Picasso, Braque, Monet (who was still alive then)—and a few writers: Joyce, Ezra, the good of Stein . . .

INTERVIEWER: When you are writing, do you ever find your-self influenced by what you're reading at the time?

HEMINGWAY: Not since Joyce was writing *Ulysses*. His was not a direct influence. But in those days when words we knew were barred to us, and we had to fight for a single word, the influence of his work was what changed everything, and made it possible for us to break away from the restrictions.

INTERVIEWER: Could you learn anything about writing from the writers? You were telling me yesterday that Joyce, for example, couldn't bear to talk about writing.

HEMINGWAY: In company with people of your own trade you ordinarily speak of other writers' books. The better the writers the less they will speak about what they have written themselves. Joyce was a very great writer and he would only explain what he was doing to jerks. Other writers that he respected were supposed to be able to know what he was doing by reading it.

INTERVIEWER: You seem to have avoided the company of writers in late years. Why?

HEMINGWAY: That is more complicated. The further you go in writing the more alone you are. Most of your best and oldest friends die. Others move away. You do not see them except rarely, but you write and have much the same contact with them as though you were together at the café in the old days. You exchange comic, cheerfully obscene and irresponsible letters, and it is almost as good as talking. But you are more alone because that is how you must work and the time to work is shorter all the time and if you waste it you feel you have committed a sin for which there is no forgiveness.

INTERVIEWER: What about the influence of some of these

people—your contemporaries—on your work? What was Gertrude Stein's contribution, if any? Or Ezra Pound's? Or Max Perkins's?

HEMINGWAY: I'm sorry but I am no good at these postmortems. There are coroners literary and non-literary provided to deal with such matters. Miss Stein wrote at some length and with considerable inaccuracy about her influence on my work. It was necessary for her to do this after she had learned to write dialogue from a book called *The Sun Also Rises*. I was very fond of her and thought it was splendid she had learned to write conversation. It was no new thing to me to learn from everyone I could, living or dead, and I had no idea it would affect Gertrude so violently. She already wrote very well in other ways. Ezra was extremely intelligent on the subjects he really knew. Doesn't this sort of talk bore you? This backyard literary gossip while washing out the dirty clothes of thirty-five years ago is disgusting to me. It would be different if one had tried to tell the whole truth. That would have some value. Here it is simpler and better to thank Gertrude for everything I learned from her about the abstract relationship of words, say how fond I was of her, reaffirm my loyalty to Ezra as a great poet and a loyal friend, and say that I cared so much for Max Perkins that I have never been able to accept that he is dead. He never asked me to change anything I wrote except to remove certain words which were not then publishable. Blanks were left, and anyone who knew the words would know what they were. For me he was not an editor. He was a wise friend and a wonderful companion. I liked the way he wore his hat and the strange way his lips moved.

INTERVIEWER: Who would you say are your literary fore-bears—those you have learned the most from?

HEMINGWAY: Mark Twain, Flaubert, Stendhal, Bach, Tur-genev, Tolstoy, Dostoyevsky, Chekhov, Andrew Marvell, John Donne, Maupassant, the good Kipling, Thoreau, Cap-tain Marryat, Shakespeare, Mozart, Quevodo, Dante, Virgil, Tintoretto, Hieronymus Bosch, Brueghel, Patinir, Goya, Giotto, Cézanne, Van Gogh, Gauguin, San Juan de la Cruz, Góngora—it would take a day to remember everyone. Then it would sound as though I were claiming an erudition I did not possess instead of trying to remember all the people who have been an influence on my life and work. This isn't an old dull question. It is a very good but a solemn question and requires an examination of conscience. I put in painters, or started to, because I learn as much from painters about how to write as from writers. You ask how this is done? It would take an-other day of explaining. I should think what one learns from composers and from the study of harmony and counterpoint would be obvious.

INTERVIEWER: Did you even play a musical instrument?

HEMINGWAY: I used to play cello. My mother kept me out of school a whole year to study music and counterpoint. She thought I had ability, but I was absolutely without talent. We played chamber music—someone came in to play the violin; my sister played the viola, and mother the piano. That cello—I played it worse than anyone on earth. Of course, that year I was out doing other things too.

INTERVIEWER: Do you reread the authors of your list? Twain, for instance?

HEMINGWAY: You have to wait two or three years with Twain. You remember too well. I read some Shakespeare every year, *Lear* always. Cheers you up if you read that.

INTERVIEWER: Reading, then, is a constant occupation and pleasure.

HEMINGWAY: I'm always reading books—as many as there are. I ration myself on them so that I'll always be in supply.

INTERVIEWER: Do you ever read manuscripts?

HEMINGWAY: You can get into trouble doing that unless you know the author personally. Some years ago I was sued for plagiarism by a man who claimed that I'd lifted *For Whom the Bell Tolls* from an unpublished screen scenario he'd written. He'd read this scenario at some Hollywood party. I was there, he said, at least there was a fellow called "Ernie" there listening to the reading, and that was enough for him to sue for a million dollars. At the same time he sued the producers of the motion pictures *Northwest Mounted Police* and the *Cisco Kid*, claiming that these, as well, had been stolen from that same unpublished scenario. We went to court and, of course, won the case. The man turned out to be insolvent.

INTERVIEWER: Well, could we go back to that list and take on one of the painters—Hieronymus Bosch, for instance? The nightmare symbolic quality of his work seems so far removed from your own.

HEMINGWAY: I have the nightmares and know about the ones other people have. But you do not have to write them down. Anything you can omit that you know you still have in the writing and its quality will show. When a writer omits things he does not know, they show like holes in his writing.

INTERVIEWER: Does that mean a close knowledge of the works of the people on your list helps fill the "well" you were speaking of a while back? Or were they consciously a help in developing the techniques of writing?

HEMINGWAY: They were a part of learning to see, to hear, to think, to feel and not feel, and to write. The well is where your "juice" is. Nobody knows what it is made of, least of all yourself. What you know is if you have it, or you have to wait for it to come back.

INTERVIEWER: Would you admit to there being symbolism in your novels?

HEMINGWAY: I suppose there are symbols since critics keep finding them. If you do not mind I dislike talking about them and being questioned about them. It is hard enough to write books and stories without being asked to explain them as well. Also it deprives the explainers of work. If five or six or more good explainers can keep going why should I interfere with them? Read anything I write for the pleasure of reading it. Whatever else you find will be the measure of what you brought to the reading.

INTERVIEWER: Continuing with just one question on this line: One of the advisory staff editors wonders about a parallel he feels he's found in *The Sun Also Rises* between the dramatis personae of the bull ring and the characters of the novel itself. He points out that the first sentence of the book tells us Robert Cohn is a boxer; later, during the *desencajonada*, the bull is described as using his horns like a boxer, hooking and jabbing. And just as the bull is attracted and pacified by the presence of a steer, Robert Cohn defers to Jake who is emasculated precisely as is a steer. He sees Mike as the picador, baiting Cohn repeatedly. The editor's thesis goes on, but he wondered if it was your conscious intention to inform the novel with the tragic structure of the bullfight ritual.

HEMINGWAY: It sounds as though the advisory staff editor was a little bit screwy. Who ever said Jake was "emasculated precisely as is a steer"? Actually he had been wounded in quite a different way and his testicles were intact and not damaged. Thus he was capable of all normal feelings as a *man* but incapable of consummating them. The important distinction is that his wound was physical and not psychological and that he was not emasculated.

INTERVIEWER: These questions which inquire into craftsmanship really are an annoyance.

HEMINGWAY: A sensible question is neither a delight nor an annoyance. I still believe, though, that it is very bad for a writer to talk about how he writes. He writes to be read by the eye and no explanations or dissertations should be necessary. You can be sure that there is much more there than will be read at any first reading and having made this it is not the writer's province to explain it or to run guided tours through the more difficult country of his work.

INTERVIEWER: In connection with this, I remember you have also warned that it is dangerous for a writer to talk about a work-in-progress, that he can "talk it out" so to speak. Why should this be so? I only ask because there are so many writers—Twain, Wilde, Thurber, Steffens come to mind—who would seem tohave polished their material by testing it on listeners.

HEMINGWAY: I cannot believe Twain ever "tested out" *Huckleberry Finn* on listeners. If he did they probably had him cut out good things and put in the bad parts. Wilde was said by people who knew him to have been a better talker than a writer. Steffens talked better than he wrote. Both his writing and his talking were sometimes hard to believe, and I heard many stories change as he grew older. If Thurber can talk as well as he writes he must be one of the greatest and least boring talkers. The man I know who talks best about his own trade and has the pleasantest and most wicked tongue is Juan Belmonte, the matador.

INTERVIEWER: Could you say how much thought-out effort went into the evolvement of your distinctive style?

HEMINGWAY: That is a long-term tiring question and if you spent a couple of days answering it you would be so self-conscious that you could not write. I might say that what amateurs call a style is usually only the unavoidable awkwardness in first trying to make something that has not heretofore been made. Almost no new classics resemble other previous classics. At first people can see only the awkwardness. Then they are not so perceptible. When they show so very awkwardly people think these awkwardnesses are the style and many copy them. This is regrettable.

INTERVIEWER: You once wrote that the simple circumstances under which various pieces of fiction were written could be instructive. Could you apply this to "The Killers"—you said that you had written it, "Ten Indians" and "Today is Friday" in one day—and perhaps to your first novel *The Sun Also Rises*?

HEMINGWAY: Let's see. *The Sun Also Rises* I started in Valencia on my birthday, July 21. Hadley, my wife, and I had gone to Valencia early to get good tickets for the *feria* there which started the twenty-fourth of July. Everybody my age had written a novel and I was still having a difficult time writing a paragraph. So I started the book on my birthday, wrote all through the *feria*, in bed in the morning, went on to Madrid and wrote there. There was no *feria* there, so we had a room with a table and I wrote in great luxury on the table and around the corner from the hotel in a beer place in the Pasaje Alvarez where it was cool. It finally got too hot to write and we went to Hendaye. There was a small cheap hotel there on the big long lovely beach and I worked very well there and then went up to Paris and finished the first draft in the apartment over the sawmill at 113 rue Notre-Dame-des-Champs six weeks from the day I started it. I showed the first draft to Nathan Asch, the novelist, who then had quite a strong accent, and he said, "Hem, vaht do you mean saying you wrote a novel? A novel huh. Hem you are writing a travel buch." I was not too discouraged by Nathan and rewrote the book, keeping in the travel (that was the best part about the fishing trip and Pamplona) at Schruns in the Voralberg at the Hotel Taube.

The stories you mention I wrote in one day in Madrid on May 16 when it snowed out the San Isidro bullfights. First I wrote "The Killers," which I tried to write before and failed. Then after lunch I got in bed to keep warm and wrote "Today Is Friday." I had so much juice I thought maybe I was going crazy and I had about six other stories to write. So I got dressed and walked to Fornos, the old bullfighters café, and drank coffee and then came back and wrote "Ten Indians." This made me very sad and I drank some brandy and went to sleep. I'd forgotten to eat and one of the waiters brought me up some *bacalao* and a small steak and fried potatoes and a bottle of Valdepeñas.

The woman who ran the pension was always worried that I did not eat enough and she had sent the waiter. I remember sitting up in bed and eating, and drinking the Valdepeñas. The waiter said he would bring up another bottle. He said the Señora wanted to know if I was going to write all night. I said no, I thought I would lay off for a while. Why don't you try to write just one more, the waiter asked. I'm only supposed to write one, I said. Nonsense, he said. You could write six. I'll try tomorrow, I said. Try it tonight, he said. What do you think the old woman sent the food up for?

I'm tired, I told him. Nonsense, he said (the word was not *nonsense*). You tired after three miserable little stories. Translate me one.

Leave me alone, I said. How am I going to write it if you don't leave me alone? So I sat up in bed and drank the Valdepeñas and thought what a hell of a writer I was if the first story was as good as I'd hoped.

INTERVIEWER: How complete in your own mind is the conception of a short story? Does the theme, or the plot, or a character change as you go along?

HEMINGWAY: Sometimes you know the story. Sometimes you make it up as you go along and have no idea how it will come out. Everything changes as it moves. That is what makes the movement which makes the story. Sometimes the movement is so slow it does not seem to be moving. But there is always change and always movement.

INTERVIEWER: Is it the same with the novel, or do you work out the whole plan before you start and adhere to it rigorously?

HEMINGWAY: *For Whom the Bell Tolls* was a problem which I carried on each day. I knew what was going to happen in principle. But I invented what happened each day I wrote.

INTERVIEWER: Were *The Green Hills of Africa, To Have and*

Have Not, and *Across the River and into the Trees* all started as short stories and developed into novels? If so, are the two forms so similar that the writer can pass from one to the other without completely revamping his approach?

HEMINGWAY: No, that is not true. *The Green Hills of Africa* is not a novel but was written in an attempt to write an absolutely true book to see whether the shape of a country and the pattern of a month's action could, if truly presented, compete with a work of the imagination. After I had written it I wrote two short stories, "The Snows of Kilimanjaro" and "The Short Happy Life of Francis Macomber." These were stories which I invented from the knowledge and experience acquired on the same long hunting trip one month of which I had tried to write a truthful account of in *The Green Hills*. To Have and Have Not and *Across the River and into the Trees* were both started as short stories.

INTERVIEWER: Do you find it easy to shift from one literary project to another or do you continue through to finish what you start?

HEMINGWAY: The fact that I am interrupting serious work to answer these questions proves that I am so stupid that I should be penalized severely. I will be. Don't worry.

INTERVIEWER: Do you think of yourself in competition with other writers?

HEMINGWAY: Never. I used to try to write better than certain dead writers of whose value I was certain. For a long time now I have tried simply to write the best I can. Sometimes I have good luck and write better than I can.

INTERVIEWER: Do you think a writer's power diminishes as he grows older? In *The Green Hills of Africa* you mention that American writers at a certain age change into Old Mother Hubbards.

HEMINGWAY: I don't know about that. People who know what they are doing should last as long as their heads last. In that book you mention, if you look it up, you'll see I was sounding off about American literature with a humorless Austrian character who was forcing me to talk when I wanted to do something else. I wrote an accurate account of the conversation. Not to make deathless pronouncements. A fair percent of the pronouncements are good enough.

INTERVIEWER: We've not discussed character. Are the characters of your work taken without exception from real life?

HEMINGWAY: Of course they are not. *Some* come from real life. Mostly you invent people from a knowledge and understanding and experience of people.

INTERVIEWER: Could you say something about the process of turning a real-life character into a fictional one?

HEMINGWAY: If I explained how that is sometimes done, it would be a handbook for libel lawyers.

INTERVIEWER: Do you make a distinction—as E. M. Forster does—between "flat" and "round" characters?

HEMINGWAY: If you describe someone, it is flat, as a photograph is, and from my standpoint a failure. If you make him up from what you know, there should be all the dimensions.

INTERVIEWER: Which of your characters do you look back on with particular affection?

HEMINGWAY: That would make too long a list.

INTERVIEWER: Then you enjoy reading over your own books—without feeling there are changes you would like to make?

HEMINGWAY: I read them sometimes to cheer me up when it is hard to write and then I remember that it was always difficult and how nearly impossible it was sometimes.

INTERVIEWER: How do you name your characters?

HEMINGWAY: The best I can.

INTERVIEWER: Do the titles come to you while you're in the process of doing the story?

HEMINGWAY: No. I make a list of titles *after* I've finished the story or the book—sometimes as many as a hundred. Then I start eliminating them, sometimes all of them.

INTERVIEWER: And you do this even with a story whose title is supplied from the text—"Hills Like White Elephants," for example?

HEMINGWAY: Yes. The title comes afterwards. I met a girl in Prunier where I'd gone to eat oysters before lunch. I knew she'd had an abortion. I went over and we talked, not about that, but on the way home I thought of the story, skipped lunch, and spent that afternoon writing it.

INTERVIEWER: So when you're not writing, you remain constantly the observer, looking for something which can be of use.

HEMINGWAY: Surely. If a writer stops observing he is finished. But he does not have to observe consciously nor think how it will be useful. Perhaps that would be true at the beginning. But later everything he sees goes into the great reserve of things he knows or has seen. If it is any use to know it, I always try to write on the principle of the iceberg. There is seven-eighths of it underwater for every part that shows. Anything you know you can eliminate and it only strengthens your iceberg. It is the part that doesn't show. If a writer omits something because he does not know it then there is a hole in the story.

The Old Man and the Sea could have been over a thousand pages long and had every character in the village in it and all the processes of how they made their living, were born, educated, bore children, et cetera. That is done excellently and well by other writers. In writing you are limited by what has already been done satisfactorily. So I have tried to learn to do something else. First I have tried to eliminate everything unnecessary to conveying experience to the reader so that after he or she has read something it will become a part of his or her experience and seem actually to have happened. This is very hard to do and I've worked at it very hard.

Anyway, to skip how it is done, I had unbelievable luck this time and could convey the experience completely and have it be one that no one had ever conveyed. The luck was that I had a good man and a good boy and lately writers have forgotten there still are such things. Then the ocean is worth writing about just as man is. So I was lucky there. I've seen the marlin mate and know about that. So I leave that out. I've seen a school (or pod) of more than fifty sperm whales in that same stretch of water and once harpooned one nearly sixty feet in length and lost him. So I left that out. All the stories I know from the fishing village I leave out. But the knowledge is what makes the underwater part of the iceberg.

INTERVIEWER: Archibald MacLeish has spoken of a method of conveying experience to a reader which he said you developed while covering baseball games back in those *Kansas City Star* days. It was simply that experience is communicated by small details, intimately preserved, which have the effect of indicating the whole by making the reader conscious of what he had been aware of only subconsciously...

HEMINGWAY: The anecdote is apocryphal. I never wrote baseball for the *Star*. What Archie was trying to remember was how I was trying to learn in Chicago in around 1920 and was searching for the unnoticed things that made emotions, such as the way an outfielder tossed his glove without looking back to where it fell, the squeak of resin on canvas under a fighter's flat-soled gym shoes, the gray color of Jack Blackburn's skin when he had just come out of stir, and other things I noted as a painter sketches. You saw Blackburn's strange color and the old razor cuts and the way he spun a man before you knew his history. These were the things which moved you before you knew the story.

INTERVIEWER: Have you ever described any type of situation of which you had no personal knowledge?

HEMINGWAY: That is a strange question. By personal knowledge you mean carnal knowledge? In that case the answer is positive. A writer, if he is any good, does not describe. He invents or *makes* out of knowledge personal and impersonal and sometimes he seems to have unexplained knowledge which could come from forgotten racial or family experience. Who teaches the homing pigeon to fly as he does; where does a fighting bull get his bravery, or a hunting dog his nose? This is an elaboration or a condensation on that stuff we were talking about in Madrid that time when my head was not to be trusted.

INTERVIEWER: How detached must you be from an experience before you can write about it in fictional terms? The African air crashes you were involved in, for instance?

HEMINGWAY: It depends on the experience. One part of you sees it with complete detachment from the start. Another part is very involved. I think there is no rule about how soon we should write about it. It would depend on how well adjusted the individual was and on his or her recuperative powers. Certainly it is valuable to a trained writer to crash in an aircraft which burns. He learns several important things very quickly. Whether they will be of use to him is conditioned by survival. Survival, with honor, that outmoded and all-important word, is as difficult as ever and as all-important to a writer. Those who do not last are always more beloved since no one has seen them in their long, dull, unrelenting no-quarter-given-and-no-quarter received, fights that they do make to do something as they believe it should be done before they die. Those who die or quit early and easy and with every good reason are preferred because they are understandable and human. Failure and well-disguised cowardice are more human and more beloved.

INTERVIEWER: Could I ask you to what extent you think the writer should concern himself with the sociopolitical problems of his times?

HEMINGWAY: Everyone has his own conscience, and there should be no rules about how a conscience should function. All you can be sure about in a political-minded writer is that if his work should last you will have to skip the politics when you read it. Many of the so-called politically enlisted writers change their politics frequently. This is very exciting to them and to their political-literary reviews. Sometimes they even have to rewrite their viewpoints . . . and in a hurry. Perhaps it can be respected as a form of the pursuit of happiness.

INTERVIEWER: Has the political influence of Ezra Pound on the segregationist Kasper had any effects on your belief that the poet ought to be released from St. Elizabeth's Hospital*?

HEMINGWAY: No. None at all. I believe Ezra should be released and allowed to write poetry in Italy on an undertaking by him to abstain from any politics. I would be happy to see Kasper jailed as soon as possible. Great poets are not necessarily girl guides nor scoutmasters nor splendid influences on youth. To name a few: Verlaine, Rimbaud, Shelley, Byron, Baudelaire, Proust, Gide should not have been confined to prevent them from being aped in their thinking, their manners or their morals, by local Kaspers. I am sure that it will take a footnote in ten years to explain who Kasper was.

INTERVIEWER: Would you say, ever, that there is any didactic intention in your work?

HEMINGWAY: Didactic is a word that has been misused and spoiled. *Death in the Afternoon* is an instructive book.

INTERVIEWER: It has been said that a writer only deals with one or two ideas throughout his work. Would you say your work reflects one or two ideas?

---

* In 1958, a Federal court in Washington, D.C., dismissed all charges against Pound, clearing the way for his release from St. Elizabeth's.

HEMINGWAY: Who said that? It sounds much too simple. The man who said it possibly *had* only one or two ideas.

INTERVIEWER: Well, perhaps it would be better put this way: Graham Greene said that a ruling passion gives to a shelf of novels the unity of a system. You yourself have said, I believe, that great writing comes out of a sense of injustice. Do you consider it important that a novelist be dominated in this way—by some such compelling sense?

HEMINGWAY: Mr. Greene has a facility for making statements that I do not possess. It would be impossible for me to make generalizations about a shelf of novels or a wisp of snipe or a gaggle of geese. I'll try a generalization though. A writer without a sense of justice and of injustice would be better off editing the yearbook of a school for exceptional children than writing novels. Another generalization. You see; they are not so difficult when they are sufficiently obvious. The most essential gift for a good writer is a built-in, shockproof, shit detector. That is the writer's radar and all great writers have had it.

INTERVIEWER: Finally, a fundamental question: as a creative writer what do you think is the function of your art? Why a representation of fact, rather than fact itself?

HEMINGWAY: Why be puzzled by that? From things that have happened and from things as they exist and from all things that you know and all those you cannot know, you make something through your invention that is not a representation but a whole new thing truer than anything true and alive, and you make it alive, and if you make it well enough, you give it immortality. That is why you write and for no other reason that you know of. But what about all the reasons that no one knows?

HEMINGWAY IN CUBA

INTERVIEW BY ROBERT MANNING
THE ATLANTIC MONTHLY
DECEMBER 1954

On the shore of Havana's back harbor a stubborn hulk rests in drydock and erodes with time. Its engine and expensive fishing tackle are gone. The fading letters of its name, *Pilar*, are still visible on the stern. "No one else should sail the *Pilar*," says Mary Hemingway. She had hoped to have it towed to sea and sunk off the port of Cojimar, deep into the fishing hole where a strike came at last to the old man "who fished alone in the Gulf Stream and had gone eighty-four days now without taking a fish." The Cuban Government's red tape prevented that, so the *Pilar* now decays in the Caribbean sun.

Ten miles from Havana, in the village of San Francisco de Paula, is Hemingway's longtime home away from home. The plantation he called Finca Vigia (Lookout Farm), with its big limestone villa and thirteen acres of banana trees, tropical shrubs, and casual gardens, stands much as he and his wife left it in 1960 when he came home to the States for the last time. It is now a Cuban Government museum. Some Cubans who ran the place for "Papa" still live and work there, caring for the grounds and the sprawling villa and pointing out to visitors the pool where "Papa" swam, the big bedroom where he wrote, and the tall white tower where he would sit to work or to stare from his heights toward the spread of Havana.

Who in my generation was not moved by Hemingway the writer and fascinated by Hemingway the maker of his own legend? "Veteran out of the wars before he was twenty," as Archibald MacLeish described him. "Famous at twenty-five; thirty a master." Wine-stained moods in the sidewalk cafés and roistering nights in Left Bank *boîtes*. Walking home alone in the rain. Talk of death, and scenes of it, in the Spanish sun. Treks and trophies in Tanganyika's green hills. Duck-shooting in the Venetian marshes. Fighting in, and writing about, two world wars. Loving and drinking and fishing out of Key West and Havana. Swaggering into Toots Shor's or posturing in *Life* magazine or talking a verbless sort of Choctaw for the notebooks of Lillian Ross and the pages of the *New Yorker*.

By the time I got the opportunity to meet him, he was savoring the highest moment of his fame—he had just won the Nobel Prize for Literature—but he was moving into the twilight of his life. He was fifty-five but looked older, and was trying to mend a ruptured kidney, a cracked skull, two compressed and one cracked vertebra, and bad burns suffered in the crash of his airplane in the Uganda bush the previous winter. Those injuries, added to half a dozen head wounds, more than 200 shrapnel scars, a shot-off kneecap, wounds in the feet, hands, and groin, had slowed him down. The casually comfortable Cuban villa had become more home than any place he'd had, and days aboard the *Pilar* were his substitute for high adventure abroad.

In a telephone conversation between San Francisco de Paula and New York, Hemingway had agreed to be interviewed on the occasion of his Nobel award, but he resisted at first because one of the magazines I worked with had recently published a penetrating article on William Faulkner. "You guys cut him to pieces, to pieces," Hemingway said. "No, it was a good piece," I said, "and it would have been even better if Faulkner had seen the writer."

"Give me a better excuse," Hemingway said, and then thought of one himself. He saw the arrival of a visitor as an opportunity to fish on the *Pilar* after many weeks of enforced idleness. "Bring a heavy sweater, and we'll go out on the boat," he said. "I'll explain to Mary that you're coming down to cut me up and feed me to William Faulkner."

A handsome young Cuban named René, who had grown up on Hemingway's place as his all-round handyman, chauffeur, and butler, was at Havana Airport to meet me and hustle my luggage, which included a batch of new phonograph records and, as a last-minute addition, a gift from Marlene Dietrich. On hearing that someone was going to Cuba to see her old friend, she sent along a newly released recording called "Shake, Rattle, and Roll," which now may be vaguely remembered as the Java man artifact in the evolution of popular rock 'n' roll. "Just like the Kraut," said Hemingway. He found the sentiment more appealing than the music.

A big man. Even after allowing for all the descriptions and photographs, the first impression of Hemingway in the flesh was size. He was barefoot and barelegged, wearing only floppy khaki shorts and a checked sport shirt, its tail tumbling outside. He squinted slightly through round silver-framed glasses, and a tentative smile, the sort that could instantly turn into a sneer or snarl, showed through his clipped white beard. Idleness had turned him to paunch, and he must have weighed then about 225 pounds, but there was no other suggestion of softness in the burly, broad-shouldered frame, and he had the biceps and calves of an N.F.L. linebacker.

"Drink?" Hemingway asked. The alacrity of the reply pleased him, and the smile broadened into a laugh. He asked René to mix martinis and said, "Thank God you're a drinking man. I've been worried ever since I told you to come down. There was a photographer here for three days a while ago who didn't drink. He was the cruelest man I've ever met. Cruelest man in the world. Made us stand in the sun for hours at a time. And he didn't drink." With stiff caution, he sank into a large overstuffed chair which had been lined back, sides, and bottom with big art and picture books to brace his injured back.

Hemingway sipped and said, "Now, if you find me talking in monosyllables or without any verbs, you tell me, because I never really talk that way. She [he meant Lillian Ross] told me she wanted to write a piece of homage to Hemingway. That's what she told me when I agreed to see her up in New York." He laughed. "I knew her for a long time. Helped her with her first big piece, on Sidney Franklin."

"I don't mind talking tonight," Hemingway said, "because I never work at night. There's a lot of difference between night thinking and day thinking. Night thoughts are usually nothing. The work you do at night you always will have to do over again in the daytime anyhow. So let's talk. When I talk, incidentally, it's just talk. But when I write I mean it for good."

The living room was nearly fifty feet long and high-ceilinged, with gleaming white walls that set off the Hemingways' small but choice collection of paintings (including a Miró, two by Juan Gris, a Klee, a Braque—since stolen from the villa—and five André Massons), a few trophy heads from the African safaris. In another room, near the entrance to a

large tile-floored dining room, was an oil portrait of Hemingway in his thirties, wearing a flowing open-collar white
shirt. "It's an old-days picture of me as Kid Balzac by Waldo
Pierce," said Hemingway. "Mary has it around because she
likes it."

He rubbed the tight-curled white beard and explained
that he wore it because when clean-shaven his skin was af-
flicted with sore spots if he spent much time in the sun. "I'll
clip the damned thing off for Christmas so as not to run
against Santa Claus," he said, "and if I rest the hide a couple of weeks at a time, I may be able to keep it off. Hope
so anyway."

In one large corner of the living room stood a six-foot-high
rack filled with dozens of magazines and newspapers from
the States, London, and Paris. In casual piles, books littered
windowsills and tables and spilled a trail into two large rooms
adjacent. One was a thirty-by-twenty-foot library whose
floor-to-ceiling shelves sagged with books. The other was
Hemingway's large but crowded bedroom study—littered
with correspondence in varied stages of attention or neglect.
There were neat piles of opened letters together with stamped
and addressed replies: cardboard boxes overflowing with the
shards of correspondence that had been opened, presumably
read, and one day might be filed; a couple of filing cabinets,
whose mysteries probably were best known to a part-time ste-
nographer the Hemingways brought in from Havana a day or
two at a time when needed. There was also a large lion skin, in
the gaping mouth of which lay half a dozen letters and a pair

of manila envelopes. "That's the Urgent in-box," Hemingway explained.

The villa seemed awash with books—nearly 400, including two dozen cookbooks, in Mary Hemingway's bedroom; more than 500, mostly fiction, history, and music, in the big sitting room; another 300, mostly French works of history and fiction, in an elegantly tiled room called the Venetian Room; nearly 2000 in the high-shelved library, these carefully divided into history, military books, biography, geography, natural history, some fiction, and a large collection of maps; 900 volumes, mostly military manuals and textbooks, history and geography in Spanish, and sports volumes, in Hemingway's bedroom. In the tall tower he kept another 400 volumes, including foreign editions of his own works, and some 700 overflowed into shelves and tabletops in the finca's small guesthouse. All the books, including Hemingway's collection of autographed works by many of his contemporaries, were impounded at the villa by the Castro regime, though Mrs. Hemingway was able to take away some of the paintings and personal belongings.

From the kitchen came sounds and smells of dinner in preparation. René emerged with two bottles of a good Bordeaux from a cellar that was steadily replenished from France and Italy. Evening sounds grew strident in the soft tropical outdoors. Distant dogs yelped. Near the house, a hoot owl broke into short, sharp cries. "That's the Bitchy Owl," Hemingway said. "He'll go on like that all night. He's lived here longer than we have.

"I respect writing very much," he said abruptly, "the writer not at all, except as the instrument to do the writing.

When a writer retires deliberately from life or is forced out of it by some defect, his writing has a tendency to atrophy, just like a man's limb when it's not used.

"I'm not advocating the strenuous life for everyone or trying to say it's the choice form of life. Anyone who's had the luck or misfortune to be an athlete has to keep his body in shape. The body and mind are closely coordinated. Fattening of the body can lead to fattening of the mind. I would be tempted to say that it can lead to fattening of the soul, but I don't know anything about the soul." He halted, broodingly, as if reflecting on his own aches and pains, his too ample paunch, a blood pressure that was too high, and a set of muscles that were suffering too many weeks of disuse. "However, in everyone the process of fattening or wasting away will set in, and I guess one is as bad as the other."

He had been reading about medical discoveries which suggested to him that a diet or regimen or treatment that may work for one man does not necessarily work for another. "This was known years ago, really, by people who make proverbs. But now doctors have discovered that certain men need more exercise than others; that certain men are affected by alcohol more than others; that certain people can assimilate more punishment in many ways than others.

"Take Primo Carnera, for instance. Now he was a real nice guy, but he was so big and clumsy it was pitiful. Or take Tom Wolfe, who just never could discipline his mind to his tongue. Or Scott Fitzgerald, who just couldn't drink." He pointed to a couch across the room. "If Scott had been drinking with us and Mary called us to dinner, Scott'd make it to his feet, all right, but then he'd probably fall down. Alcohol

was just poison to him. Because all these guys had these weak-
nesses, it won them sympathy and favor, more sometimes
than a guy without those defects would get."

For a good part of his adult life Hemingway was, of
course, a ten-goal drinker, and he could hold it well. He was
far more disciplined in this regard, though, than the legend
may suggest. Frequently when he was working hard, he would
drink nothing, except perhaps a glass or two of wine with
meals. By rising at about daybreak or half an hour thereafter,
he had put in a full writing day by ten or eleven in the morning and was ready for relaxation when others were little more
than under way.

As in his early days, Hemingway in the late years worked
with painful slowness. He wrote mostly in longhand, frequently while standing at a bookcase in his bedroom; occasionally he would typewrite ("when trying to keep up with
dialogue"). For years he carefully logged each day's work. Except for occasional spurts when he was engaged in relatively
unimportant efforts, his output ran between 400 and 700
words a day. Mary Hemingway remembers very few occasions
when it topped 1000 words. He did not find writing to be
quick or easy. "I always hurt some," he remarked.

Hemingway was capable of great interest in and generosity toward younger writers and some older writers, but as he shows
in *A Moveable Feast* (written in 1957–1959 and finished in the
spring of 1961), he had a curious and unbecoming compul-
sion to poke and peck at the reputations of many of his literary contemporaries. Gertrude Stein, Sherwood Anderson,

T. S. Eliot, not to mention Fitzgerald, Wolfe, Ford Madox Ford, James Gould Cozzens, and others, were invariably good for a jab or two if their names came up. As for the critics— "I often feel," he said, "that there is now a rivalry between writing and criticism, rather than the feeling that one should help the other." Writers today could not learn much from the critics. "Critics should deal more with dead writers. A living writer can learn a lot from dead writers."

Fiction-writing, Hemingway felt, was to invent out of knowledge. "To invent out of knowledge means to produce inventions that are true. Every man should have a built-in automatic crap detector operating inside him. It also should have a manual drill and a crank handle in case the machine breaks down. If you're going to write, you have to find out what's bad for you. Part of that you learn fast, and then you learn what's good for you."

What sort of things? "Well, take certain diseases. These diseases are not good for you. I was born before the age of antibiotics, of course . . . Now take *The Big Sky* [by A. B. Guthrie]. That was a very good book in many ways, and it was very good on one of the diseases . . . just about the best book ever written on the clap." Hemingway smiled.

"But back to inventing. In *The Old Man and the Sea* I knew two or three things about the situation, but I didn't know the story." He hesitated, filling the intervals with a vague movement of his hands. "I didn't even know if that big fish was going to bite for the old man when it started smelling around the bait. I had to write on, inventing out of knowledge. You reject everything that is not or can't be completely true. I didn't know what was going to happen for sure in *For Whom the Bell Tolls* or *Farewell to Arms*. I was inventing."

Philip Young's *Ernest Hemingway*, published in 1953, had attributed much of Hemingway's inspiration or "invention" to his violent experiences as a boy and in World War I.

"If you haven't read it, don't bother," Hemingway volunteered. "How would you like it if someone said that everything you've done in your life was done because of some trauma. Young had a theory that was like—you know, the Procrustean bed, and he had to cut me to fit into it."

During dinner, the talk continued on writing styles and techniques. Hemingway thought too many contemporary writers defeated themselves through addiction to symbols. "No good book has ever been written that has in it symbols arrived at beforehand and stuck in." He waved a chunk of French bread. "That kind of symbol sticks out like—like raisins in raisin bread. Raisin bread is all right, but plain bread is better."

He mentioned Santiago, his old fisherman, in roughly these terms: Santiago was never alone because he had his friend and enemy, the sea, and the things that lived in the sea, some of which he loved and others he hated. He loved the sea, but the sea is a great whore, as the book made clear. He had tried to make everything in the story real—the boy, the sea, and the marlin and the sharks, the hope being that each would then mean many things. In that way, the parts of a story become symbols, but they are not first designed or planted as symbols.

•

The Bitchy Owl hooted the household to sleep. I was awakened by tropical birds at the dawn of a bright and promising day. This was to be Hemingway's first fishing trip on *Pilar* since long before his African crash. By six thirty he was dressed in yesterday's floppy shorts and sport shirt, barefooted, and hunched over his *New York Times*, one of the six papers he and Mary read every day. From the record player came a mixture of Scarlatti, Beethoven, Oscar Peterson, and a remake of some 1928 Louis Armstrong.

At brief intervals Hemingway popped a pill into his mouth. "Since the crash I have to take so many of them they have to fight among themselves unless I space them out," he said.

While we were breakfasting, a grizzled Canary Islander named Gregorio, who served as the *Pilar*'s first mate, chef, caretaker, and bartender, was preparing the boat for a day at sea. By nine o'clock, with a young nephew to help him, he had fueled the boat, stocked it with beer, whiskey, wine, and a bottle of tequila, a batch of fresh limes, and food for a large seafood lunch afloat. As we made out of Havana Harbor, Gregorio at the wheel and the young boy readying the deep-sea rods, reels, and fresh bait-fish, Hemingway pointed out landmarks and waved jovially to passing skippers. They invariably waved back, occasionally shouting greetings to "Papa." He sniffed the sharp sea air with delight and peered ahead for the dark line made by the Gulf Stream. "Watch the birds," he said. "They show us when the fish are up."

Mary Hemingway had matters to handle at the finca and in the city, so she could not come along, but out of concern for Hemingway's health she exacted a promise. In return for the long-missed fun of a fishing expedition, he agreed to take it easy and to return early, in time for a nap before an art exhibit to which he and Mary had promised their support. He was in a hurry, therefore, to reach good fishing water. Gregorio pushed the boat hard to a stretch of the Gulf Stream off Cojimar. Hemingway relaxed into one of the two cushioned bunks in the boat's open-ended cabin.

"It's wonderful to get out on the water. I need it." He gestured toward the ocean. "It's the last free place there is, the sea. Even Africa's about gone; it's at war, and that's going to go on for a very long time."

The *Pilar* fished two rods from its high antenna-like outriggers and two from seats at the stern, and at Hemingway's instruction, Gregorio and the boy baited two with live fish carefully wired to the hooks, and two with artificial lures. A man-o'-war bird gliding lazily off the coast pointed to the first school of the day, and within an hour the *Pilar* had its first fish, a pair of bonito sounding at the end of the outrigger lines. Before it was over, the day was to be one of the best fishing days in many months, with frequent good runs of bonito and dolphin and pleasant interludes of quiet in which to sip drinks, to soak up the Caribbean sun, and to talk.

Sometimes moody, sometimes erupting with boyish glee at the strike of a tuna or the golden blue explosion of a hooked dolphin, and sometimes—as if to defy or outwit his wounds—pulling himself by his arms to the flying bridge to steer the *Pilar* for a spell, Hemingway talked little of the present, not at all of the future, and a great deal of the past.

He recalled when Scribner's sent him first galley proofs of *For Whom the Bell Tolls*. "I remember, I spent ninety hours on the proofs of that book without once leaving the hotel room. When I finished, I thought the type was so small nobody would ever buy the book. I'd shot my eyes, you see. I had corrected the manuscript several times but still was not satisfied. I told Max Perkins about the type, and he said if I really thought it was too small, he'd have the whole book reprinted. That's a real expensive thing, you know. He was a sweet guy. But Max was right, the type was all right."

"Do you ever read any of your stuff over again?"

"Sometimes I do," he said. "When I'm feeling low. It makes you feel good to look back and see you can write."

"Is there anything you've written that you would do differently if you could do it over?"

"Not yet."

New York. "It's a very unnatural place to live. I could never live there. And there's not much fun going to the city now. Max is dead. Granny Rice is dead. He was a wonderful guy. We always used to go to the Bronx Zoo and look at the animals."

The Key West days, in the early thirties, were a good time. "There was a fighter there—he'd had one eye ruined, but he was still pretty good, and he decided to start fighting again. He wanted to be his own promoter. He asked me if I would referee his bout each week. I told him, 'Nothing doing,' he shouldn't go in the ring anymore. Any fighter who knew about his bad eye would just poke his thumb in the other one and then beat his head off.

"The fighter said, 'The guys come from somewhere else won't know 'bout my eye, and no one around here in the Keys gonna dare poke my eye.'

"So I finally agreed to referee for him. This was the Negro section, you know, and they really introduced me: 'And the referee for tonight, the world-famous millionaire, sportsman, and playboy, Mister Ernest Hemingway!'" Hemingway chuckled. "Playboy was the greatest title they thought they could give a man." Chuckle again. "How can the Nobel Prize move a man who has heard plaudits like that?"

Frequently a sharp cry from Gregorio on the flying bridge interrupted the talk. "Feesh! Papa, feesh!" Line would snap from one of the outriggers, and a reel begin to snarl. "You take him," Hemingway would say, or if two fish struck at once, as frequently happened, he would leap to one rod and I to the other.

For all the hundreds of times it had happened to him, he still thrilled with delight at the quivering run of a bonito or the slash of a dolphin against the sky. "Ah, beautiful! A beautiful fish. Take him softly now. Easy. Easy. Work him with style. That's it. Rod up slowly. Now reel in fast. *Suave! Suave!* Don't break his mouth. If you jerk, you'll break his mouth, and the hook will go."

When action lulled, he would scan the seascape for clues to better spots. Once a wooden box floated in the near distance, and he ordered Gregorio toward it. "We'll fish that box," he said, explaining that small shrimp seek shelter from the sun beneath flotsam or floating patches of seaweed and these repositories of food attract dolphin. At the instant the lures of the stern rods passed the box, a dolphin struck and was hooked, to be pumped and reeled in with the heavy-duty glass rod whose butt rested in a leather rod holder strapped around the hips.

He talked about the act of playing a fish as if it were an English sentence. "The way to do it, the style, is not just an idle concept. It is simply the way to get done what is supposed to be done; in this case it brings in the fish. The fact that the right way looks pretty or beautiful when it's done is just incidental."

Hemingway had written only one play, *The Fifth Column*. Why no others?

"If you write a play, you have to stick around and fix it up," he said. "They always want to fool around with them to make them commercially successful, and you don't like to stick around that long. After I've written, I want to go home and take a shower."

Almost absently, he plucked James Joyce out of the air. "Once Joyce said to me he was afraid his writing was too suburban and that maybe he should get around a bit and see the world, the way I was doing. He was under great discipline, you know—his wife, his work, his bad eyes. And his wife said, yes, it was too suburban. 'Jim could do with a spot of that lion-hunting.' How do you like that? A *spot* of lion-hunting!

"We'd go out, and Joyce would fall into an argument or a fight. He couldn't even see the man, so he'd say, 'Deal with him, Hemingway! Deal with him!'" Hemingway paused. "In the big league it is not the way it says in the books."

Hemingway was not warm toward T. S. Eliot. He preferred to praise Ezra Pound, who at that time was still confined in St. Elizabeth's mental hospital in Washington. "Ezra Pound is a great poet, and whatever he did, he has been punished greatly, and I believe should be freed to go and write poems in Italy, where he is loved and understood. He was the master of Eliot. I was a member of an organization which Pound founded with Natalia Barney in order to get Eliot out of his job in a bank so he could be free to write poetry. It was called Bel Esprit. Eliot, I believe, was able to get out of his job and edit a review and write poetry freely due to the backing of other people than this organization. But the organization was typical of Pound's generosity and interest in all forms of the arts regardless of any benefits to himself or of the possibilities that the people he encouraged would be his rivals.

"Eliot is a winner of the Nobel Prize. I believe it might well have gone to Pound, as a poet. Pound certainly deserved punishment, but I believe this would be a good year to release poets and allow them to continue to write poetry…. Ezra Pound, no matter what he may think, is not as great a poet as Dante, but he is a very great poet for all his errors."

Dusk was coming when the *Pilar* turned toward Havana Harbor, its skipper steering grandly from the flying bridge. What remained of the bottle of tequila and a half of lime rested in a holder cut into the mahogany rail near the wheel. "To ward off sea serpents," Hemingway explained, passing the bottle for a ceremonial homecoming swig.

At the docks, René reported that the gallery opening had been postponed. Hemingway was overjoyed. "Now we can relax for a while and then get some sleep. We went out and had a good day and got pooped. Now we can sleep."

Hemingway's good spirits on his return helped to diminish his wife's concern about his over-extending himself. She served up a hot oyster stew, and later, clutching an early nightcap, Hemingway sprawled with pleased fatigue in his big armchair and talked of books he had recently read. He had started Saul Bellow's *The Adventures of Augie March*, but didn't like it. "But when I'm working," he said, "and read to get away from it, I'm inclined to make bad judgments about other people's writing." He thought Bellow's very early book, *Dangling Man*, much better.

One of the post-war writers who had impressed him most was John Horne Burns, who wrote *The Gallery* and two other novels and then, in 1953, died in circumstances that suggested suicide. "There was a fellow who wrote a fine book and then a stinking book about a prep school, and then he just blew himself up," Hemingway mused, adding a gesture that seemed to ask, How do you explain such a thing? He stared at nothing, seeming tired and sad.

"You know," he said, "my father shot himself."

There was silence. It had frequently been said that Hemingway never cared to talk about his father's suicide.

"Do you think it took courage?" I asked.

Hemingway pursed his lips and shook his head. "No. It's everybody's right, but there's a certain amount of egotism in it and a certain disregard of others." He turned off that conversation by picking up a handful of books. "Here are a few things you might like to look at before you turn off the light." He held out *The Retreat*, by P. H. Newby, Max Perkins's selected letters, *The Jungle Is Neutral*, by Frederick S. Chapman, and Malcolm Cowley's *The Literary Situation*.

By seven the next morning a rabble of dogs yipped and yelped in the yard near the finca's small guesthouse. René had been to town and returned with the mail and newspapers.

Hemingway, in a tattered robe and old slippers, was already half through the *Times*.

"Did you finish the Cowley book last night?" he asked. "Very good, I think. I never realized what a tough time writers have economically, if they have it as tough as Malcolm says they do."

He was reminded of his early days in Paris. "It never seemed like hardship to me. It was hard work, but it was fun. I was working, and I had a wife and kid to support. I remember, first I used to go to the market every morning and get the stuff for Bumby's [his first son, John] bottle. His mother had to have her sleep." Lest this should be taken as a criticism, he added, "That's characteristic, you know, of the very finest women. They need their sleep, and when they get it, they're wonderful."

Another part of the routine in the Paris days, to pick up eating money, was Hemingway's daily trip to a gymnasium to work as a sparring partner for fighters. The pay was two dollars an hour. "That was very good money then, and I didn't get marked up very much. I had one rule: never provoke a fighter. I tried not to get hit. They had plenty of guys they could knock around."

He reached for the mail, slit open one from a pile of fifteen letters. It was from a high school English teacher in Miami, Florida, who complained that her students rarely read good literature and relied for "knowledge" on the movies, television, and radio. To arouse their interest, she wrote, she told them about Hemingway's adventures and pressed them to read his writings. "Therefore, in a sense," she concluded, "you are the teacher in my tenth grade classroom. I thought you'd like to know it." Hemingway found the letter depressing: "Pretty bad if kids are spending all that time away from books."

The next fishing expedition was even better than the first—fewer fish, but two of them were small marlin, one about eighty pounds, the other eighty-five, that struck simultaneously and were boated, Hemingway's with dispatch, the second at a cost of amateurish sweat and agony that was the subject of as much merriment as congratulations. It was a more sprightly occasion, too, because Mary Hemingway was able to come along. A bright, generous, and energetic woman, Hemingway's fourth wife cared for him well, anticipated his moods and his desires, enjoyed and played bountiful hostess to his friends, diplomatically turned aside some of the most taxing demands on his time and generosity. More than that, she shared his love and the broad mixture of interests—books, good talk, traveling, fishing, shooting—that were central to Hemingway's life. His marriage to her was plainly the central and guiding personal relationship of his last fifteen years.

Hemingway gazed happily at the pair of marlin. "We're back in business," he said, and gave Mary a hug. "This calls for celebration," said Mary.

"Off to the Floridita," said Hemingway.

The Floridita was once one of those comfortably shoddy Havana saloons where the food was cheap and good and the drinking serious. By then, enjoying a prosperity that was due in no small part to its reputation as the place you could see and maybe even drink with Papa Hemingway, it had taken on a red-plush grandeur and even had a velvet cord to block off the dining room entrance. "It looks crummy now," Hemingway said, "but the drinking's as good as ever."

The Floridita played a special role in Hemingway's life. "My not living in the United States," he explained, "does not mean any separation from the tongue or even the country. Any time I come to the Floridita I see Americans from all over. It can even be closer to America in many ways than being in New York. You go there for a drink or two, and see everybody from everyplace. I live in Cuba because I love Cuba—that does not mean a dislike for anyplace else. And because here I get privacy when I write. If I want to see anyone, I just go into town, or the Air Force guys come out to the place, naval characters and all—guys I knew in the war. I used to have privacy in Key West, but then I had less and less when I was trying to work, and there were too many people around, so I'd come over here and work in the Ambos Mundos Hotel."

The Floridita's bar was crowded, but several customers obligingly slid away from one section that had been designated long before by the proprietor as "Papa's Corner." Smiles. "Hello, Papa." Handshakes all around. "Three Papa Dobles," said Hemingway, and the barkeep hastened to manufacture three immense daiquiris according to a Floridita recipe that relies more on grapefruit juice than on lemon or lime juice. The Papa Doble was a heavy seller in those days at $1.25, and a bargain at that.

Two sailors off a U.S. aircraft carrier worked up nerve to approach the author and ask for an autograph. "I read all your books," said one of them.

"What about you?" Hemingway said to the other.

"I don't read much," the young sailor said.

"Get started," Hemingway said.

The Floridita's owner appeared, with embraces for the Hemingways and the news that he was installing a modern men's room. Hemingway noted sadly that all the good things were passing. "A wonderful old john back there," he said. "Makes you want to shout: Water closets of the world unite; you have nothing to lose but your chains."

There were some other chances in later years to talk with Hemingway, in Cuba and New York, and there were a few letters in between—from Finca Vigia or Spain or France, or from Peru, where he went to fish with the Hollywood crew that made the film of *The Old Man and the Sea*. "Here's the chiropractor who fixed up my back," said the inscription on a postcard-size photograph from Peru showing him and an immense marlin he landed off Puerto Blanco.

Trips to New York grew less frequent and did not seem to amuse or entertain him. Unlike the old days and nights at Shor's or Twenty-one, he later usually preferred to see a few friends and dine in his hotel suite. Top health never really seemed to come back to him. He was having trouble with his weight, blood pressure, and diet. He was still working, though, as the stylishly written pages of *A Moveable Feast* show. (How much else he was producing then is not clear. Mrs. Hemingway, together with Scribner's and Hemingway's authorized biographer, Carlos Baker, and his old friend Malcolm Cowley, is sifting a trunkload of manuscripts that include some short stories, several poems, some fragments of novels, and at least one long completed novel about the sea—written to be part of a trilogy about land, sea, and air.)

His curiosity about the world, about people, about the

old haunts (that word probably ought to be taken both ways) remained zestful, and so did his willingness to talk books and authors.

Once NBC did an hour-long radio documentary featuring recollections by many people who knew Hemingway, including some who were no longer friends. Sidney Franklin's comments annoyed him. "I never traveled with Franklin's bullfighting 'troupe,'" Hemingway said. "That is all ballroom bananas. I did pay for one of his operations, though, and tried to get him fights in Madrid when no promoter would have him, and staked him to cash so he wouldn't have to pawn his fighting suits." Max Eastman had retold on the broadcast his version of the memorable fight between him and Hemingway at Scribner's over Eastman's reflections on whether Hemingway really had any hair on his chest. "He was sort of comic," said Hemingway. "There used to be a character had a monologue something like 'Listen to What I Done to Philadelphia Jack O'Brien.' Eastman is weakening though. In the original version he stood me on my head in a corner, and I screamed in a high-pitched voice."

Hemingway added: "None of this is of the slightest importance, and I never blow the whistle on anyone, nor dial N for Narcotics if I find a friend or enemy nursing the pipe."

On a later occasion, a dean of theology wrote in the *New Republic* an article entitled "The Mystique of Merde" about those he considered to be "dirty" writers, and put Hemingway near the top of his list. A newsmagazine reprinted part of the article, and when he read it, Hemingway, then in Spain, addressed as a rebuttal to the dean a hilarious short lecture on the true meaning of the word *merde* and its use as a word of honor among the military and theatrical people. It is, Hemingway explained, what all French officers say to one another when going on an especially dangerous mission or to their deaths, instead of *au revoir*, good-bye, good luck old boy, or any similar wet phrases. "I use old and bad words when they are necessary, but that does not make me a dirty writer," he said. For the dean, he had a dirty word. But he did not send the note to him; the writing of it turned his irritation into a shrug.

The Hemingways left Cuba in July of 1960 and went to Key West. From there, with luggage that filled a train compartment, they went to New York to live for a while in a small apartment. Later they moved to the new place Hemingway had bought in Ketchum, Idaho, close to the kind of shooting, fishing, walking that had beguiled him as a young boy in upper Michigan. He went to Spain for six weeks that summer to follow his friend Ordoñez and his rival, Dominguin, in their in their *mano a mano* tour of bullfights and to write *The Dangerous Summer*, bullfight pieces commissioned by *Life* magazine. I have the impression that he didn't think very much of them, but he didn't say. His spirits seemed low after that and ostensibly stayed that way, though he apparently kept at work out in Ketchum almost until the day his gun went off.

The rereading of the notes and letters from which these glimpses of Hemingway are drawn—for glimpses are all they are—induces a curious thought: It is possible that to have known him, at least to have known him superficially and late in his life, makes it more rather than less difficult to understand him.

He made himself easy to parody, but he was impossible to imitate. He sometimes did or said things that seemed almost perversely calculated to obscure his many gallantries and generosities and the many enjoyments and enthusiams he made possible for others. He could be fierce in his sensitivity to criticism and competitive in his craft to the point of vindictiveness, but he could laugh at himself ("I'm Ernie Hemorrhoid, the poor man's Pyle," he announced when he put on his war correspondent's uniform) and could enjoy the pure pride of believing that he had accomplished much of what he set out to do forty-five years before in a Parisian loft.

The private Hemingway was an artist. The public Hemingway was an experience, one from which small, sharp remembrances linger as persistently as the gusty moments:

A quiet dinner in New York when he remarked out of a rueful silence, and with a hint of surprise, "You know—all the beautiful women I know are growing old."

A misty afternoon in Cuba when he said, "If I could be something else, I'd like to be a painter."

A letter from the clinic in Rochester, Minnesota, where doctors were working him over: he reported "everything working o.k."—the blood pressure down from 250/125 to 130/80, and the weight down to 175 pounds, low for that big frame. He was two months behind, he said, on a book that was supposed to come out that fall—the fall of 1961.

And last of all, a Christmas card with the extra message in his climbing script: "We had fun, didn't we?"

DROPPING IN ON HEMINGWAY

INTERVIEW BY LLOYD LOCKHART
THE STAR WEEKLY MAGAZINE
APRIL 1958

"You've come to my house without permission," he said quietly. "It's not right."

I said I was from *The Star Weekly* where he once worked.

"It's not right," he said, "but c'mon in."

Havana, Cuba

Ernest Hemingway is "the aging herd bull of American literature." Matador, soldier, war correspondent, espionage agent, author, big game hunter, fisherman, raconteur, bon vivant—his life has been phenomenal. And Cuba is his springboard. He lives at Francisco de Paulo, a few miles outside Havana.

The word was out that "the great one" (they don't call him "papa" down here) was hard at work on a new book. That meant no visitors. Of course, Hemingway has been more or less inaccessible for five years anyway—ever since he staggered out of the African jungle, carrying a bunch of bananas and a bottle of gin, after two successive plane crashes.

Remember his memorable statement of survival? "My luck, she is running good," he said. And he has been running from newspapermen ever since.

A ragged row of houses leads to the Hemingway estate where a big sign on the gate says: "No admittance except by appointment." I had no appointment but I went in anyway. I had tried to telephone the great one from Toronto—no dice. I had written a letter—no answer. Friends had tried to mediate—no result. This was my last chance—personal contact.

Hemingway owns 13 acres with an asphalt drive leading to his Spanish-style villa. It was 2 p.m. and I had a letter in my hand—the direct appeal type thing that reporters hate to use. I expected a servant would answer or Mrs. Hemingway (she's No. 4). She screens her husband from all visitors.

Anyway, I knocked, then peeked through the screen. I could see a big shape sitting at the table, in silhouette, with a spade-like blob dropping from the chin. It was Hemingway eating lunch. He came to the door puzzled and a bit hurt.

"You've come to my house without permission," he said quietly. "It's not right."

I said I was from *The Star Weekly*, the paper he once worked for, and that I tried to telephone.

"It's not right," he repeated. "I'm working on a book and I don't give interviews. I want that understood. But c'mon in."

We entered the living room.

"I know you're disappointed, but I'm not being rude, am I?" he said. "If I give an interview to you, 20 others would want to know why I broke my rule. That isn't rude, is it? How about coffee? Maybe a drink?"

We settled on coffee and now, for the first time, I saw Hemingway in clear light. Amazing man! Incredible! He has a Neptune-like beard, flopped-back silver hair, tremendous physique. Is he only 59? It's hard to believe. He looks 20 years older. Yet his huge brown eyes have glitter, and when he grins—boom!—he's a kid.

"I feel good," Hemingway said. "That plane business took something out of me but I got it all back. I fractured my skull and broke a couple of ribs. They healed. They always do."

He was wearing brown fishing pants, blue sneakers and a fire-engine red shirt—working togs, apparently, because he'd just come down from "the tower." That's where he does his writing, standing by a mantelpiece doing narrative in longhand, but typing dialogue "to keep it running."

"People don't realize I'm a professional writer—that I write to earn my living," he said. "Everybody who comes to Cuba knows I'm here so they drop out for a chat, if I let them. In winter it's impossible. Are you a Woodbine man? Well, you know how horses put on weight during layoffs—they get fat and sleek. It's the same with me. I have to take weight off in winter, so I do it by writing."

How was the book going?

"It goes according to concentration—that's why I don't give interviews," he said. "One fellow came down here and kept interrupting me to clear up parts of his story. When I read over what I had written I could tell to the paragraph when he arrived and when he left. He destroyed my concentration."

Hemingway paused to sip his coffee.

"When you're a writer," he said, "you got to keep it going, because when you've lost it God knows when you'll get it back."

I noticed several portraits of him hanging in the room.

"The picture I like best was done by Karsh—you know him, good fellow from Ottawa," he said. "He came in here and took his pictures without any trouble. Other photographers arrive with strobe equipment, three or four cameras. They upset me completely. So do interviewers. I can't apply myself to answering questions. I've tried, but I can't. What I have to say I put in writing. I'm no philosopher. I have nothing I can say in words."

Then Hemingway got back to why I was there.

"No, I won't give an interview—it wouldn't be fair," he said. "You wouldn't believe the way I've been burned, the things they've written about me that weren't true. I remember landing in Paris with Mary (Mrs. Hemingway) and giving a press conference in a friendly, courteous fashion. Well, one reporter asked where we were headed and I told him Mont St. Michel. As it turned out, Mary and I changed our minds—we went straight to Paris. Guess what? The following day a Paris newspaper had a two-page story telling how this reporter had gone with us to Mont St. Michel, reporting conversations he had with me, making up quotes all by himself."

Hemingway—and this may surprise some people—is a shy, modest he-man. True, he has covered umpteen wars and has the wounds and medals to prove it. True, he has been gored by a bull, charged by elephants, exhausted by giant fish. True, he has conducted vicious feuds, his consumption of alcohol is legendary, his search for adventure has covered the world. Yet—though it seems remarkable—he never uses the word "I" with bravado, and the only time he smiles is at his failings. He even underrates his newspaper career.

"Editors seemed to think I was good at interviews when I wasn't at all," he said. "I didn't like asking personal questions which were none of my business and that's what interviewers are supposed to do."

Why does Hemingway live in Cuba? That question has been asked a thousand times. His invariable answer:

"I have good luck writing in Cuba. First, I used to come over from Key West when there weren't many people around and I'd work at a small hotel near the waterfront. I'd get up at daylight, work, then go out in a boat and fish.

"I moved over from Key West in 1938 and bought this place when *For Whom the Bell Tolls* came out. I wake at dawn to work, then I sit in the sun and have a drink and read the papers. I miss going around to the joints and seeing the boys, but I lost about five years' work out of my life during the war and I'm trying to make it up. I can't work and hang around New York because I never learned how to do it. When I hit New York it's like somebody coming off a long cattle drive in the old days into Dodge City."

In case anybody gets the idea he's being snobbish or aloof living in Cuba, the great one adds: "Find me a place in Canada where I can live on top of a hill and be 15 minutes from the Gulf Stream and have my own fruit and vegetables year round and raise and fight game chickens without breaking the law and I'll go live in Canada if Mary and her cats and dogs will agree."

I asked Hemingway if he'd changed much since he worked on *The Star Weekly* back in the early '20's.

"I've changed—we all do. It has to happen," he said. "If I knew then what I know now I would have written my books under an assumed name. I don't want to be famous. I don't like publicity. All I ask from life is to write, hunt, fish, and be obscure. Fame embitters me. Questions torture me. I've had reporters submit lists of questions asking what I think of life . . . that type of thing. It would take days to answer."

"How exactly have you changed?" I asked.

"I used to argue a lot. I had strong opinions about everything and anything," he said. "Now I've learned to keep quiet, to let other people do the talking. I listen to what they say… unless I think they're lying. Then I say something to find out for sure. I've decided talking serves no purpose . . . not for me. If you know a subject well, why talk about it? If you don't know a subject, why make a fool of yourself?

"The reason I've become bitter," he said, "is because I don't know whom I can trust. I've had reporters call me on the telephone and, though I haven't said anything, they've written long stories. Just try to get me on the telephone today! My wife screens all calls and I insist on knowing exactly what they're about before I take over. I have had to do that. It's the only way."

The great man swigged off his coffee and shook himself to his feet. I got the hint. The interview that wasn't an interview was over.

"Say hello to anybody who knows me in Toronto. I wasn't rude, now, was I?" he said. "I didn't kick you out. Please understand my position."

"Mr. Hemingway," I said, "I'm sorry I didn't get an interview but if I had, there's one question I would have asked: What is your formula for getting the most out of life?"

He thought about it for maybe a second.

"Never look for excitement—let excitement come to you," was his answer.

LIFE IN THE AFTERNOON: THE LAST INTERVIEW

INTERVIEW BY ROBERT EMMETT GINNA

ESQUIRE

MAY 1958

In May 1958, I arrived in Havana, bent on talking with Ernest Hemingway and hopeful of persuading him to appear on television as the subject of an interview. (I was then the producer of a series called, rather loftily, *Wisdom*, in which eminent men and women of great accomplishment and seminal influence were interviewed at home about their life and work.) Hemingway had long been sought, but although there had been correspondence over a period of time, he had shied away. Accordingly, one day I had packed, as a sample, the film of an interview already made with Igor Stravinsky and a magnum of Château Latour, 1937—a claret and vintage of magnificence—and boarded a flight for Cuba.

On a sultry Cuban afternoon I was driven out to San Francisco de Paula, a village not many miles from Havana. The gates to Hemingway's home—Finca Vigia—were locked, and I handed my driver Luis some money and told him to scout around and get them opened; some local would have a key to let in tradespeople. In a few minutes we drove in and around the circular drive to the low, white house, deep in green foliage, a modest looking but commodious Spanish colonial farmhouse.

Although I had called from the Ambos Mundos the day before Mrs. Hemingway had been evasive. She said that Hemingway was working terribly hard and should not see any callers. She promised, however, to call me after I explained that I had only wanted to present him the Stravinsky film. But she hadn't, and I was determined to deliver it, together with the wine and a personal note saying that the bottle was purely a gift from me to him with thanks.

I peered through the screen door and, hearing nothing nor seeing anyone within the heavily shaded house, I tried the door, thinking just to put my packages and note inside. In a moment a familiar figure appeared at the door. Hemingway was wearing somewhat tattered shorts, a sport shirt out at the waist, and no shoes. He asked me in, and I introduced myself, handing him the package of film, the wrapped bottle and the note, which he put on a table in the entranceway. Politely, in the soft but high voice which surprised so, coming from a man of his scale, he asked me to sit down, leading the way into the spacious, informally furnished living room, along the white plaster walls on which were low, overflowing bookcases. His behavior was almost painfully shy. Motioning me to a deep chair beside a tray groaning with bottles, he took one opposite. Apologetically, he said that he was terribly hard at work, that it was going well, and that he hadn't supposed that anything very good would come of my calling on him. With a certain diffidence, he repeated his familiar arguments about being unwilling to speak about writing, that talking about it killed it, "took something from it," "made it go away," "spooked" him.

I assured him that I understood, but that we still wanted to record him for the future. He demurred, and I asked him if he hadn't got something from visiting and talking with established writers like Sherwood Anderson when he was only an aspiring writer in Chicago, before departing for France.

"Oh, but we never spoke of writing," replied Hemingway—pronouncing the word distinctly as if it were spelled *wright-ing*. "Anderson told stories. He loved to tell stories, and he told them well. But he wouldn't talk about writing; not then. It wouldn't have worked. Later he was different. But I only saw him maybe four or five times.

"You take Joyce. He would never talk about his writing. Oh, maybe after he had finished something. *Ulysses*. He would explain some of those things later. He would read aloud. He had a nice voice and read well."

"Joyce had a beautiful tenor voice," I said.

"A nice voice," said Hemingway. "But if you came to talk about writing, he would only stare at you. He was nasty."

"He was rather cynical," I said.

"Not cynical. Nasty. But he was nice," said Hemingway.

He returned to the theme that he could not talk about his own work. He paused and looked at me over the tops of his steel-rimmed spectacles, his brown eyes pale and aged by time, and wild, and perhaps some of the things they had seen and he had done. "You see, I choke up when I talk about it. If I have to say anything, it has to be clearly written out." (The lengthy and perceptive interview subsequently published in *The Paris Review* was done with Hemingway carefully writing and rewriting many of his replies.)

"I have a little recording—perhaps the disc was pirated"—I said, "of your remarks to a radio correspondent upon the occasion of your notification of the Nobel Prize. You insisted then that writing was something that could not be done—at least by you—if you talked about it."

"That is public," said Hemingway. "It is what I would have said, if I had appeared for the award." Then, reflectively, he added, "I've lost so much time, 1940 to 1944, for instance, then that nonsense in Africa." He referred to the 1954 plane crash in which he was injured.

"The literary world is always speculating about the major book that you are supposed to have had in work for a long time," I said.

"I've got a bunch of stuff," Hemingway said obliquely, motioning to a room off the spacious living room.

I tried again. "Isn't this the big book that . . ."

"It's a novel," he cut in, "and I'm trying to finish it. I want to go to Spain and Africa." He paused and asked if I would have a drink. Guiltily, I rose and said that I felt like an interloper.

"No, no," he said. "I thought that you were my son Jack. I'd knocked off work. Stay a little while."

When I had sat down again, Hemingway inquired about my job, remarking that it must be a pretty good one. I told him something about it and, when he had asked me some more about myself, remarked that I was a journalist by trade and that I had kept a hand in freelancing; that, in fact, he might be amused by a little feature I was assembling—on the ten greatest bars in the world—for *Esquire*.

"For *Esquire*? The ten greatest bars in the world?" Hemingway shook his head. "How could anybody work that out?" he asked, going right on. "Well, there's the Ritz, Paris; Harry's Bar, Venice; Costello's, New York; La Floridita here. The Floridita used to be nice. Open and airy with good cross-ventilation. But the bartenders are good. The food is good, too, but expensive. It's a nice place.

"*Esquire*," he said again. "I used to work for them. In the beginning for about two years. Gingrich, now the publisher, then the editor, came down and conned me. He's a pretty good conman." Then, with the courteous afterthought characteristic of him, Hemingway added, "A nice guy, too. They paid me $1,000 for 'The Snows of Kilimanjaro.'"

"That was pretty good then, 1936," I said.

"Yes," Hemingway nodded agreeably, "but I was getting about a dollar a word then. Do you know how they used to get me? They used to print the cover and put me—my name—on it, then leave the form open. I'd have to fill it. That's how they got that ['The Snows of Kilimanjaro']. What a con-man gimmick! But I don't feel bitter."

"Gingrich is a pretty keen fisherman," I said.

"I started him," said Hemingway. "But they do put out a pretty good book. I guess they call it that now, don't they?" he said, suddenly flashing that beacon-sized smile as if to signal our partnership in knowledge about this conceit of the magazine industry. "I keep up down here," he added, pointing at an elaborate magazine rack in the entrance hall of the house, which was filled with a large variety of periodicals.

Noticing a book—Jacques Maritain's *Reflections on America*—on the table behind the two slip-covered, old, over-stuffed chairs in which we sat, I remarked, "You may be happy to know . . ."

"My publisher sent it to me," he interjected, following my glance.

". . . that Jacques Maritain has steadily declined to let us film one of these conversations," I continued.

The big smile flashed again.

"There is an interview with you coming out in *The Paris Review*. Isn't there?" I asked.

"Next month," he said, with some embarrassment. "George Plimpton kept after me for three years. Finally I did it. It took me about five or six weeks. You have to be goddamn sure what you're saying."

"I found a collection of those interviews in book form, *Writers at Work*, pretty interesting," I said.

"Yeah?" he said, warming up. "Some pretty good. But," he learned forward confidentiality, "what a lot of bull—, too. How some of those guys can believe themselves. Jesus! But there is some pretty good stuff in that book. Simenon is good. We're lucky to have him. The way he writes, huh? All those books, and his saying that he doesn't know how they're going to turn out? How does he think anybody else writes? But when he talks about his *serious* books, his strong points, why they're just the wrong things—all the things wrong with Simenon. But when he just *writes*, he's good."

"Simenon's kind of a writing machine," I said.

"A writing machine," said Hemingway. "It all goes in, and it all come out. And Dottie Parker," he murmured, apparently referring to the interview with her published in the same volume, but he didn't go on.

"I would have like to have known her in the old *Vanity Fair* days," I said, "with Bob Benchley and Robert Sherwood . . ."

"Bob Sherwood," Hemingway spoke the name, his voice dropping, barely audible, his gaze far away.

I felt myself for a moment like a sailor talking with the wind, but I went on. "There were some funny things developed in a few of those interviews. Isn't it funny how E.M. Forster, having been so analytical of writing, seemed to go out like a candle so long ago?"

"Yes, went out like a candle," Hemingway echoed again, his shaggy grey-white head bobbing assent. "Sure you can't have a drink?"

I stood up swiftly. "No, I feel bad coming by and taking up your time."

"No! Stay a while," he said. "I'm through working. I was just waiting for Jack. Have a drink."

"I will if you'll join me," I said.

"I'm having wine," he said.

"All right," I said. "That's fine by me."

Hemingway motioned toward the strong spirits on the tray beside me, and I shook my head. "May I excuse myself first?" I said, getting up.

He rose and directed me. I noticed the stand-up working place where he did his writing, the top of a bookcase near the double bed, supporting a reading board on which he usually writes, and a typewriter which he uses when he is working rapidly. The room also contained a large desk littered with newspapers, books and various gimcracks like any boy's or Franklin D. Roosevelt's, bar bells on the floor, some African trophies on the walls, a lesser kudu skin on the floor. Like everything about the house, his room had the air of long-lived-in, unpretentious comfort; it exhaled the immediate presence of an inhabitant who is at once literary and the man of action. Scribbled on the bathroom walls were numerous notations of diastolic and systolic blood pressures.

When I re-entered the living room, the host was

returning with a bottle and ice: a large high shouldered man with the bulging calves of an athlete, thin ankles and big feet, lumbering forward, padding across the cool yellow tile floor. He served the wine and ice.

"Marques de Riscal," I said, recognizing the good Spanish red wine.

"Would you prefer sherry?" asked Hemingway courteously.

I said, "No," and he gave me ice and took some himself and we drank the red wine cool, as many Europeans do and as American wine pretenders abhor.

We talked of mutual friends and Venice, and I asked if there was any good shooting there that was public.

"It's not public, but I used to get a guide in Torcello, the last time was 1950, and we would work up the canals (those through the countryside) jump-shooting at passers."

"What are passers?" I asked.

The huge smile gleamed, then Hemingway laughed. "Any damn thing that flies by! They have many species that we have—teal, widgeon, pintails, some mallards, and, sure geese, plenty of geese at the end."

We were talking of Africa and Spain when Hemingway paused and, speaking carefully, said: "The work is going pretty good. I get started at seven o'clock, have breakfast at about eight-thirty, get back to work at nine, stop for lunch and then hit it again after lunch. I'm writing too much a day. Today, a thousand words. Too much. I've got to hold myself down. But I'm trying to get finished. I want to go to Spain and Africa."

Taking up the conversation about Spain, Hemingway

said, "I made a documentary film once, myself—*The Spanish Earth*, 1937. I wrote it, but Archie MacLeish and John Dos Passos were supposed to have done it. I think I was a grip too."

Since he had mentioned movies, I said, "Your work hasn't made out too well in the movies for the most part."

"Jesus!" said Hemingway. "Usually I couldn't have anything to do with the pictures, or didn't want to. The properties had usually been sold or resold."

"*The Snows of Kilimanjaro* came out as a lot of hokum on the screen," I said.

"My ex-wife had got that property," he said. "It was sold to Hollywood long ago for something awfully small, and I never got anything out of the picture or had anything to do with it. I have lent a hand with *The Old Man and the Sea*, though, mostly trying to get the big marlin, but even there didn't make out so well. I don't know."

By this time it was nearly dark. Hemingway had shown me about and passed the time with great hospitality, and I felt that I had to leave; besides I was anxious to put my journal in order. This time I insisted on rising and walked into the entrance hall. Hemingway protested kindly and followed me. He referred to the television project that had brought me and said that primitive peoples believed that if their pictures were taken they surrendered their personal power, their *E'lan Vital*, to those who possessed their images. (Hemingway was to write to me later: "I am superstitious about being filmed or televised. Feel about it the way that certain tribes do and so haven't done it, but good luck to you and to the other characters that it does no harm to.")

I told him that I had encountered this belief among the people of the outer Fiji Islands.

He smiled delightedly and clapped me on the shoulder. Then he looked at me and said humorously, "You know that you can't buy the principles of a lifetime with a bottle?"

"Read the note later on," I replied.

"Well, if anybody ever lands me for a filmed interview, it should be you," he said. "Maybe if I can get ahead, you know, like a pitcher gets ahead so that he can coast, maybe I'll do it. Or, if I get real bad. Oh, that's a stupid way to talk. Jeez, I'm sorry you brought this bottle. What is it?"

I told him.

"Jesus," said Hemingway. "I'll need an occasion."

"It's just from me to you with thanks, no strings," I said. "It won't go on the expense account. I came down here expressly to see you."

"I feel bad," he said. "But you're having some fun in town at night, I hope?"

"I've loved every minute of it," I said.

Hemingway seemed pleased to hear it, and, laughing, hand upon my shoulder, saw me to my waiting car. "I didn't mean what I said about Joyce," he said. "About coming to the door and just staring. Why don't you meet me at La Floridita tomorrow, mid-afternoon? Will it be alright if I bring something and write something in it?"

"Just please have a look at the Stravinsky film I've left you," I said. "He is pretty entertaining, and I think the television ordeal will look fairly painless, even fun."

"Yeah, he's a ham," said Hemingway, waving goodbye.

By two-thirty the next afternoon I was installed at the

bar of La Floridita, grateful for the cool quiet of the place and the majestic frozen daiquiri in my hand. (The drink was popularized there, and though they blend many kinds, the secret of their best is a teaspoonful of maraschino in the elixir.) I sat in the corner at the front beneath the bearded bronze bust of Ernest Hemingway.

After a while Papa and Miss Mary came in. Mrs. Hemingway had a daiquiri, and Hemingway asked for Scotch with a bit of crushed lemon and a little ice. Just then Hemingway's oldest son Jack (by his first wife, Hadley Richardson) came in. I found him to be an extremely attractive and affable chap. He had been living in Cuba for some time, and although his profession of stockbroker struck me as an improbable one for the son the Ernest Hemingway, I quickly realized he shared his father's interests in the outdoor life.

When Jack and Miss Mary became engaged in a splinter conversation, I told Hemingway that my own passion for trout fishing had begun with reading his two-part story, the "Big Two-Hearted River," many years ago; that, in fact, while serving in the Navy in the South Pacific, I had read and reread it (in *The Fifth Column and the First Forty-Nine Stories*) and had dreamed about the dark and quiet waters of the Michigan north country and young Nick Adams, alone, fishing for trout. I recalled how the exactly drawn atmosphere of the story with Nick's dread of going into the dark swamp—"the fishing would be tragic. In the swamp fishing was a tragic adventure. Nick did not want it." I spoke the lines to him, there in La Floridita. I thought but did not remark how often the presence of tragedy hovered beyond the streams or bars of Hemingway's stories.

"Oh, that was just bait fishing," he said. "It doesn't really count as trout fishing." His voice and whole manner were suddenly embarrassed, I think, in trying not to appear affected, which he was, by his own words given back and the sincerity which was there, a suddenly tangible thing, between us after my doubtless terribly gauche reader-to-author remark.

My allusion to the Navy led Hemingway into several military observations, then literary ones. "There were a lot of good Navy books, I think. Of course *The Caine Mutiny* and a bunch of others, too, were—. What—, huh?"

He asked me what books about the last war I had liked and I mentioned the *The Gallery* by John Horne Burns and Norman Mailer's *The Naked and the Dead.*

"Crap," he said. "Imagine a general not looking at the coordinates. He would last long. Mailer's was no real general. Crap." All this was said in the same quiet voice. Then, as I was to note his doing several times when he was moved to temper some harsh judgment, he added, "I ought to read it again. I might feel different, huh? You think it's good?"

Hemingway's modesty about many subjects that afternoon was at variance with tales told of him, but, although aware that this was scant acquaintance, I found it convincing enough. Not long before I had been talking with Van Wyck Brooks, the distinguished American literary historian, and he had said it seemed to him that Hemingway had never grown up, that he seemed permanently adolescent in his concern for "playing soldiers" and that in this respect he was perhaps typically American and, fine stylist though he was, he was less than one of the greatest writers. Brooks had said something else, too, about Robert Cohn, the touchy Jewish-American character of Hemingway's *The Sun Also Rises* (I cannot remember now what Brooks said or precisely what I said to Hemingway on this point; certainly I did not quote Brooks' remark, but I have noted down Hemingway's rejoinder). I said something about Brooks and then something about Cohn.

"Brooks thinks I'm a bum," commented Hemingway. "Well, if he wants to call me a bum, that's alright. He's entitled to. He did good work, huh? All that work about all those authors. But, Jesus Christ, who made him—Cohn—say and stand for those things?" (Harold Loeb, the author, has written that he was the original of Robert Cohn and that Hemingway, rather too painfully for Loeb, pretty much put him down on paper.)

The afternoon was waning, drinks came and went, but Hemingway partook sparingly of his special mix. I found the chance to return to the topic of the "big book."

"Look," he said, "what I have written is my family's money in the bank. Supposing I was to publish everything I had. Imagine what it would do to taxes! I've got some stuff put away."

I asked him whether *The Old Man and the Sea* was the book about "the sea, about life" which he had been reported to have been working on over a period of time.

"Hell, no," he said. "You're talking about the big one, about war, about life." He leaned close over the bar. "I had blood poisoning when I wrote *The Old Man*. I wrote it right off in a few weeks. I wrote it for a dame; she didn't think I had it left in me. I guess I showed her. I hope so. There was a woman behind each of my books."

I was startled by his apparent candor, but maybe the

whole afternoon at the long bar, the big frozen daiquiris slid-ing down leaving a numbness for a minute had something to do with my passive mood. Hemingway said a few other things that shocked me; he spoke with bitterness about one of his family, but even then he spoke in a tone of reason, the more troubling for its conviction. Hemingway clearly loved talk-ing, but he didn't *make* talk, and I have wondered since if he meant to shock, took any pleasure in it; I didn't think so then.

Miss Mary gently interrupted our discourse to suggest that perhaps they should be getting back to the finca. Heming-way took out of an envelope a copy of a fine English edition of *The Old Man and the Sea*, beautifully illustrated with draw-ings by C.F. Tunnicliffe and Raymond Sheppard. Inside the flyleaf he had inscribed a friendly note. I was touched and grateful, but when I tried to thank him he busied himself with the bartender, having two drinks prepared for the ride back to his farm. Then we all made our farewells and he and Miss Mary went out to their open car, to sit up in the back seat and be chauffeured out to the country, drinks in hand.

Jack had gone off and I stayed on a while, finishing my drink.

"That's quite a guy," a young U.S. airman said, and I replied, "That's the truth," and hurried back to my writing table.

Hemingway and I talked again briefly, in New York. In the Autumn of 1959, from Spain, where he was once more following the bulls, Hemingway wrote, "Take care of yourself so we can have another drink at La Floridita." I wish it could have been that way.

ERNEST HEMINGWAY was raised in Oak Park, Illinois, the child of a physician and a musician. After high school, he became a journalist with *The Kansas City Star*, before enlisting to be an ambulance driver in World War I. He returned home after a serious injury in 1918, but his military experience informed his fiction, especially *A Farewell to Arms*. He worked as a war correspondent for *The Toronto Star* during his first marriage, and over the next three marriages he would live in Paris, London, Key West, and Cuba. He published seven novels, six short story collections, and two nonfiction titles. On safari in Africa in 1952 he survived two plane crashes, though his obituaries ran prematurely. He lived on to win the Nobel Prize in Literature in 1954. Two trunks of his early work from Paris reappeared in 1957, and inspired him to write his memoir *A Moveable Feast*. He committed suicide in Idaho in 1961.

GEORGE PLIMPTON was the editor of *The Paris Review* from its founding in 1953 until his death in 2003.

ROBERT MANNING was the editor in chief of *The Atlantic Monthly* from 1966 until 1980.

LLOYD LOCKHART was a reporter and photographer for *The Toronto Star*.

ROBERT EMMETT GINNA has written for *Connoisseur*, *Esquire*, and *The New York Times* and was formerly editor in chief of Little, Brown, an imprint of Hachette Book Group.

THE LAST INTERVIEW SERIES

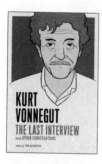

KURT VONNEGUT: THE LAST INTERVIEW

"I think it can be tremendously refreshing if a creator of literature has something on his mind other than the history of literature so far. Literature should not disappear up its own asshole, so to speak."

$15.95 / $17.95 CAN
978-1-61219-090-7
ebook: 978-1-61219-091-4

LEARNING TO LIVE FINALLY: THE LAST INTERVIEW
JACQUES DERRIDA

"I am at war with myself, it's true, you couldn't possibly know to what extent . . . I say contradictory things that are, we might say, in real tension; they are what construct me, make me live, and will make me die."

translated by PASCAL-ANNE BRAULT and MICHAEL NAAS

$15.95 / $17.95 CAN
978-1-61219-094-5
ebook: 978-1-61219-032-7

ROBERTO BOLAÑO: THE LAST INTERVIEW

"Posthumous: It sounds like the name of a Roman gladiator, an unconquered gladiator. At least that's what poor Posthumous would like to believe. It gives him courage."

translated by SYBIL PEREZ and others

$15.95 / $17.95 CAN
978-1-61219-095-2
ebook: 978-1-61219-033-4

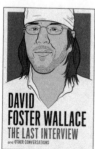

DAVID FOSTER WALLACE: THE LAST INTERVIEW

"I don't know what you're thinking or what it's like inside you and you don't know what it's like inside me. In fiction . . . we can leap over that wall itself in a certain way."

$15.95 / $15.95 CAN
978-1-61219-206-2
ebook: 978-1-61219-207-9

THE LAST INTERVIEW SERIES

JORGE LUIS BORGES: THE LAST INTERVIEW

"Believe me: the benefits of blindness have been greatly
exaggerated. If I could see, I would never leave the
house, I'd stay indoors reading the many books that
surround me."

translated by KIT MAUDE

$15.95 / $15.95 CAN
978-1-61219-204-8
ebook: 978-1-61219-205-5

HANNAH ARENDT: THE LAST INTERVIEW

"There are no dangerous thoughts for the simple reason
that thinking itself is such a dangerous enterprise."

$15.95 / $15.95 CAN
978-1-61219-311-3
ebook: 978-1-61219-312-0

RAY BRADBURY: THE LAST INTERVIEW

"You don't have to destroy books to destroy a culture.
Just get people to stop reading them."

$15.95 / $15.95 CAN
978-1-61219-421-9
ebook: 978-1-61219-422-6

JAMES BALDWIN: THE LAST INTERVIEW

"You don't realize that you're intelligent
until it gets you into trouble."

$15.95 / $15.95 CAN
978-1-61219-400-4
ebook: 978-1-61219-401-1

THE LAST INTERVIEW SERIES

GABRIEL GÁRCIA MÁRQUEZ: THE LAST INTERVIEW

"The only thing the Nobel Prize is good for is not having to wait in line."

$15.95 / $15.95 CAN
978-1-61219-480-6
ebook: 978-1-61219-481-3

LOU REED: THE LAST INTERVIEW

"Hubert Selby. William Burroughs. Allen Ginsberg. Delmore Schwartz . . . I thought if you could do what those writers did and put it to drums and guitar, you'd have the greatest thing on earth."

$15.95 / $15.95 CAN
978-1-61219-478-3
ebook: 978-1-61219-479-0